my first picture dictionary

Written by Colin Clark

Illustrated by Vivienne Bray

Brown Watson

ENGLAND

Aa

acrobat
An **acrobat** does jumping and balancing tricks.

actor
An **actor** pretends to be another person in a film or a play.
The children are **acting**.

address
The **address** on a letter says where you live.
You live at your **address**.

aircraft

An **aircraft** is a machine that flies in the sky.

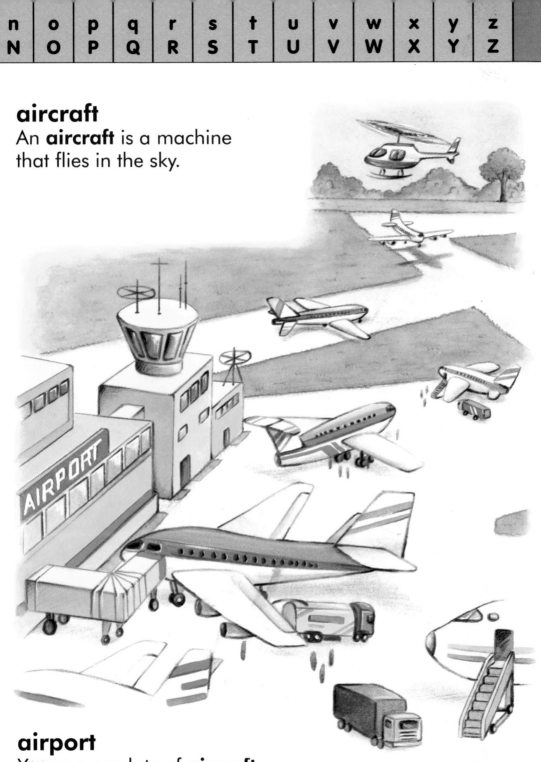

airport

You can see lots of **aircraft** landing and taking off at an **airport**.

alphabet

All the words that we speak or write are made up of the letters of the **alphabet**.

ambulance

An **ambulance** takes sick people to hospital.

animals

Any living thing that can move about and feel is called an **animal**.
Here are some pictures of **animals**.

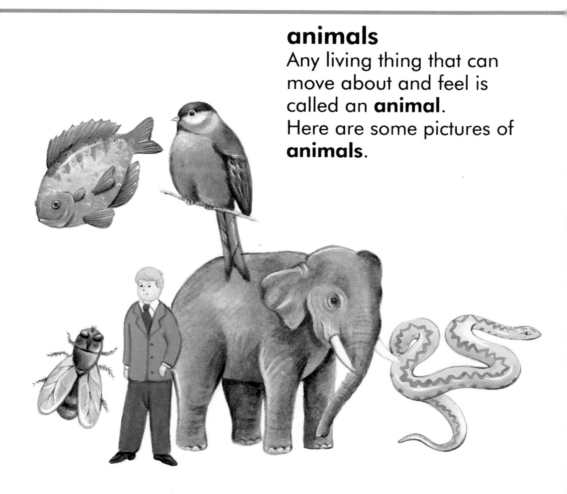

ankle
The **ankle** is the part of our body that joins the leg to the foot.

apple
An **apple** is a fruit.
Apples are good to eat, and they are good for us.

apron
When someone is cooking, they wear an **apron** to keep their clothes clean.

arm
Your **arm** is between your shoulder and your hand.
We have two **arms**.

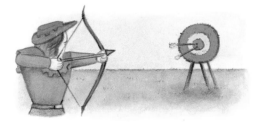

arrow
An **arrow** is fired through the air from a bow.
The head of an **arrow** is very sharp.

artist

The person painting the
picture is called an **artist**.

astronaut

An **astronaut** is someone
who travels out into space.
Some **astronauts** have been
to the Moon.

axe

An **axe** is a sharp tool
for cutting wood.
Jack cut down the beanstalk
with an **axe**.

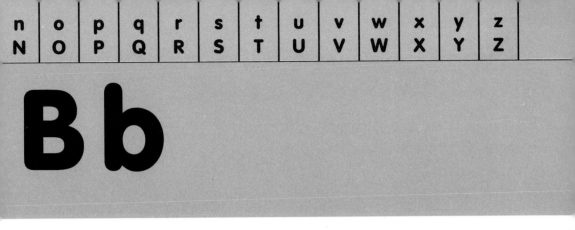

B b

baby

A **baby** is a very young child.
Babies crawl about on their hands and knees.

back

The children are standing **back** to **back**. The **backs** of their bodies are touching.

badge

The boy has a **badge** on his jumper.

bag

You can carry lots of things in a **bag**.

a	b	c	d	e	f	g	h	i	j	k	l	m
A	B	C	D	E	F	G	H	I	J	K	L	M

ball

Some games are played with a **ball**. **Balls** can be different shapes and sizes.

balloon

We blow a **balloon** full of air. We have **balloons** at parties.

banana

A **banana** is a fruit. We peel off the yellow skin before we eat a **banana**.

band

A **band** is a group of people who make music together. This **band** is playing loudly.

barn

Farmers keep their cows and hay in a **barn**.

basket

The man has a large **basket** of flowers.

bat

This flying animal is a **bat**.

In some games, we hit a ball with a **bat** like this.

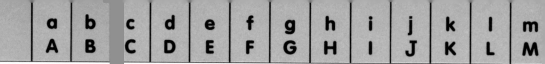

a	b	c	d	e	f	g	h	i	j	k	l	m
A	B	C	D	E	F	G	H	I	J	K	L	M

bath

We wash ourselves all over in the **bath**.

beach

The sandy part beside the sea is called the **beach**.

bear

A **bear** is a large, furry, wild animal.

bed
We lie down in a **bed** when we want to sleep.

bee
A **bee** is a buzzing insect. **Bees** live in a hive and make honey.

bell
A **bell** rings when it is time to go into school.

berry
A **berry** is a juicy fruit with little seeds in it.

bicycle
We can ride a **bicycle**. A **bicycle** has two wheels.

bird

A **bird** is an animal with
wings and feathers.
Most **birds** can fly.
Here are some **birds**.

black

Black is a very dark colour.
The hat is **black**.

blue

Blue is a colour.
The sky is **blue** and so
are the balloons.

boat

You travel over water in a **boat**.
The children are in a rowing **boat**.

book

This girl is reading a **book**. 'My First Picture Dictionary' is a **book**.

boot

A **boot** covers part of the leg as well as the foot. When it rains, we wear rubber **boots**.

bottle

A **bottle** holds something wet, like water, or milk, or lemonade, or tomato sauce.

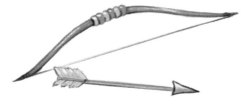

bow
We use a **bow** for shooting arrows.

boy
A male child is a **boy**.

bridge
We use a **bridge** to cross over something, like a road, a railway, or a river.

brown
Brown is a colour.
The coat is **brown**.
So is the Teddy bear.

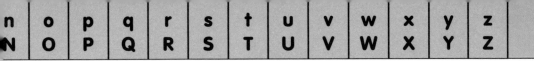

n	o	p	q	r	s	t	u	v	w	x	y	z
N	O	P	Q	R	S	T	U	V	W	X	Y	Z

brush

We use a **brush** for painting or cleaning.
We **brush** our hair.

bulldozer

A **bulldozer** can move piles of earth or rubble.

bus

A **bus** can carry people along the road. The children are in a school **bus**.

butterfly

A **butterfly** is an insect with four large wings. Some **butterflies** are very colourful.

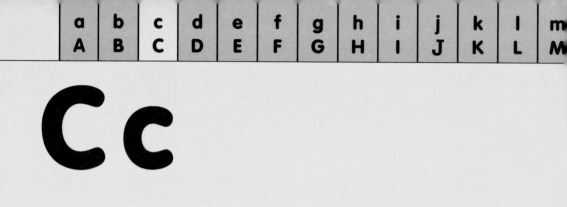

Cc

cage
Sometimes we keep pet birds or mice in a **cage**.

cake
A **cake** is sweet and baked in the oven. On our birthday, we have a birthday **cake**.

camel
A **camel** is an animal with one or two humps on its back. **Camels** live in the desert.

candle
A **candle** gives us light.

car

We travel by **car** along the road.

castle

A **castle** is a large, old building with thick stone walls and towers.

cat

A **cat** is a furry animal. We keep **cats** as pets.

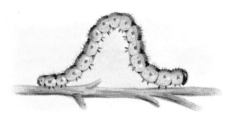

caterpillar

A **caterpillar** is long and soft, with lots of legs. A **caterpillar** changes into a moth or a butterfly.

cherry

A **cherry** is a small, round, tasty fruit. **Cherries** are sweet and good to eat.

chicken

A **chicken** is a bird. These baby **chickens** are called chicks.

chimney

The smoke from the fire goes up the **chimney**.

Christmas

December 25th is **Christmas**, the birthday of Jesus. We give presents at **Christmas**.

clock
A **clock** shows us the time.

clothes
All the things we wear are
called **clothes**.

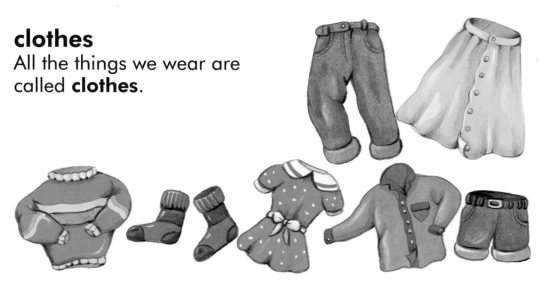

cot
A baby sleeps in a little bed
called a **cot**.

cow
A **cow** is an animal that
gives us milk.

a	b	c	d	e	f	g	h	i	j	k	l	m
A	B	C	D	E	F	G	H	I	J	K	L	M

crab

A **crab** lives in the sea.
Crabs can nip you
with their claws.

crane

A **crane** is a machine which
lifts large, heavy things.

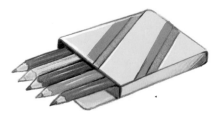

crayon

We can use a **crayon** to
colour a drawing.

cup

We drink something out of
a **cup**.

Dd

dancer
A **dancer** moves about in time to music.

deer
Deer are shy, wild animals.

dentist
A **dentist** is someone who helps us to keep our teeth shining and healthy.

desk

We can sit at a **desk** when we want to read or write.

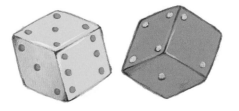

dice

We use a **dice** to play some games. A **dice** has six sides.

dinosaur

A **dinosaur** is an animal that lived a long, long time ago. Some **dinosaurs** were big and fierce.

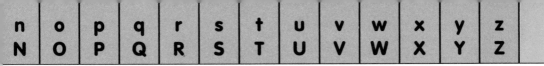

n	o	p	q	r	s	t	u	v	w	x	y	z
N	O	P	Q	R	S	T	U	V	W	X	Y	Z

doctor
When we are sick, a **doctor** will take care of us.

dog
A **dog** is a friend.
Some **dogs** are big, and some are small.

doll
A **doll** is a toy that looks like a person. We can play with a **doll**.

donkey
A **donkey** is an animal with long ears.
Donkeys say: 'Hee-Haw'.

door
A room or a cupboard has a **door**. We can open and close a **door**.

dragon

In fairy-tales, a **dragon** is a fire-breathing animal with wings.

dress

A girl or a woman will wear a **dress**.

drum

We can make music with a **drum** by hitting it with **drum**sticks.

duck

A **duck** says: 'Quack, quack'. **Ducks** are birds that can swim and fly.

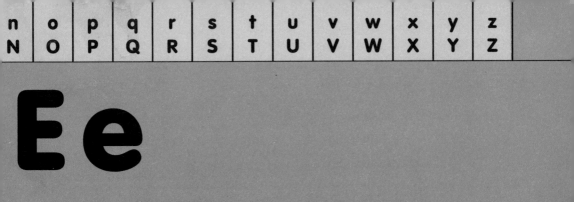

n	o	p	q	r	s	t	u	v	w	x	y	z
N	O	P	Q	R	S	T	U	V	W	X	Y	Z

E e

eagle
An **eagle** is a big bird with strong claws. **Eagles** make their nests in high places.

ear
On each side of our head, we have an **ear**.
We hear with our **ears**.

eggs
Birds and some other animals lay **eggs**.
We can eat some **eggs**.

elbow
Our arms bend in the middle at the **elbow**.

elephant

An **elephant** is a large, grey animal with big ears, and a very long nose, called a trunk.

empty

The box is **empty**.
There is nothing in the box.

end

The **end** is the last of something. Each dog has an **end** of the rope.

envelope

When we have written a letter, we put it into an **envelope** before we post it.

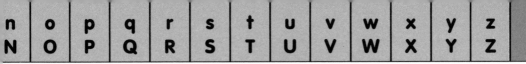

Eskimo

An **Eskimo** lives in a very cold part of the world. **Eskimos** have to wear warm, furry clothes.

exercises

The children are doing **exercises**. **Exercises** are special movements to keep our bodies fit.

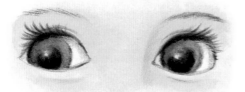

eye

The **eye** is the part of our body through which we see. We have two **eyes**.

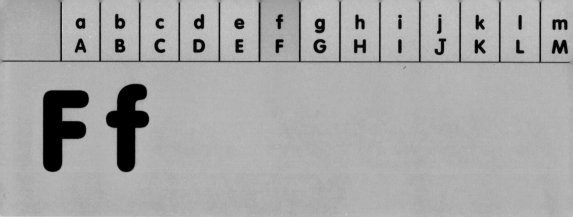

F f

face

The **face** is on the front of the head.

fair

We can have lots of fun at a **fair**.

farm

On a **farm**, food is grown and **farm** animals are kept.

feather

A **feather** is very light.
Feathers grow on birds.

fence

You put a **fence** of wood or
wire round your garden.

finger

A **finger** is a part of the
hand. On each hand, we
have four **fingers** and a
thumb.

fire

When something is burning,
there is **fire**. A **fire** is very
hot.

fish

A **fish** is an animal that lives
in water.

flag

A **flag** is a coloured piece of cloth or paper. This is the pirates' **flag**.

flowers

Flowers are pretty to look at and they smell nice.
A **flower** is the part of a plant with seeds in it.

food

Food is what we eat. Everything needs **food** to stay alive.

foot

At the end of each leg, we have a **foot**. We stand on our **feet**.

forest

There are lots of trees in a **forest**.

fountain

A **fountain** shoots water up into the air.

fox

A **fox** is a kind of wild dog, with a bushy tail.

frog

A **frog** is a small animal that lives near water. **Frogs** croak and jump, and they have webbed feet.

fruit

Some plants have **fruit**. We eat lots of **fruit**, like oranges, bananas, strawberries, and pineapples.

full

When you cannot get any more into something, it is **full**.

funny

The clown makes the children laugh. They think the clown is **funny**.

G g

garage
The car is in the **garage**.

garden
A **garden** is some land on which we grow grass and flowers. We can play in the **garden**.

gate
A **gate** is like a door in a fence. We open the **gate** to get into the garden.

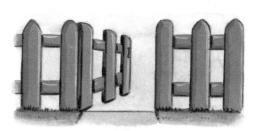

giant
A **giant** is a big person in a fairy-tale.

giraffe
A **giraffe** is a wild animal with long legs and a very long neck.

girl
A female child is a **girl**.

gloves
We wear **gloves** to keep our hands warm.

goat

A **goat** is like a large sheep with horns and a beard.

goldfish

We keep **goldfish** as pets in a tank, or in a pond in the garden.

grass

Grass is green, and grows almost everywhere. We have to cut the **grass** in the garden.

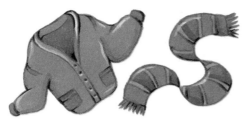

green

Green is a colour. The jumper is **green**. So is the scarf.

grey

Grey is a colour. Clouds are **grey** when it is raining.

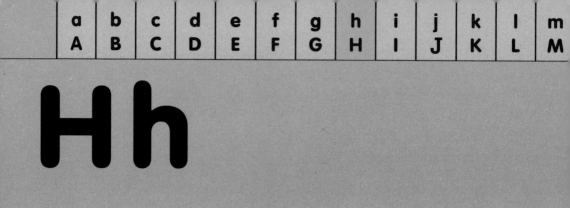

a	b	c	d	e	f	g	h	i	j	k	l	m
A	B	C	D	E	F	G	H	I	J	K	L	M

Hh

hammer
A **hammer** is a tool for banging in nails.

hamster
A **hamster** is a small, furry pet. **Hamsters** keep food in their cheeks.

hand
We have a **hand** at the end of each arm. Our **hands** are for holding and touching things.

handkerchief
We use a **handkerchief** to wipe our nose when we have a cold.

harp

We pluck the strings on a **harp** to make music.

hat

We wear a **hat** on our head.
This is a man's **hat**.

hay

Farmers store dried grass, called **hay**, for feeding cows and sheep.

head

Our **head** is on our shoulders. The face is the front of the **head**.

hedge

A **hedge** is a row of bushes which makes a fence round a field or garden.

heel

The **heel** is the back part of the foot.

helicopter

A **helicopter** is an aircraft without wings.
Helicopters can fly straight up into the air.

helmet

A **helmet** is a strong cover for the head. We wear a **helmet** to keep our head safe.

hen

A female bird is called a **hen**. We can eat the eggs of farmyard **hens**.

hill

A **hill** is higher than the land around it. **Hills** are not as high as mountains.

hook

We can hang a coat on a **hook**.

horns

Horns are the hard, pointed bits on the heads of deer. A rhino has a **horn** on its nose.

horse

A **horse** is an animal which is used for riding, or for pulling carts.

hospital

When we are very sick, we have to go to **hospital**.

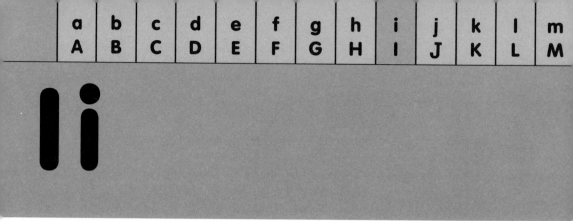

iceberg
A very large block of ice which floats in the sea is an **iceberg**.

ice cream
Ice cream is cold and sweet. Eating **ice cream** is great.

icicles
Icicles are pointed spikes of frozen water.

icing
Icing is the sweet topping put on birthday cakes.

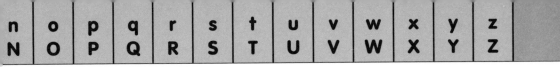

n	o	p	q	r	s	t	u	v	w	x	y	z
N	O	P	Q	R	S	T	U	V	W	X	Y	Z

igloo

Eskimos live in houses called **igloos**. An **igloo** is made from frozen snow.

insects

Insects are small animals with six legs. Some **insects** are small, some are big.

iron

We can press clothes with an **iron**.

island

An **island** is a piece of land with water all round it.

J j

jack-in-the-box
When you open the lid of a **jack-in-the-box**, a funny toy jumps out at you.

jar
We can keep sweets in a **jar**.

jeans
Jeans are trousers made from strong blue cloth.

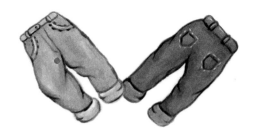

jelly
Jelly is a cold, clear, sweet pudding.

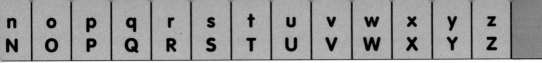

n	o	p	q	r	s	t	u	v	w	x	y	z
N	O	P	Q	R	S	T	U	V	W	X	Y	Z

jellyfish

A **jellyfish** lives in the sea.
Jellyfish look as if they are
made of jelly.

jigsaw

We have to fit together the
pieces of a **jigsaw** puzzle.

juggler

A **juggler** throws and
catches lots of things all at
once. He **juggles** things in
the air.

jumper

A knitted pullover with long
sleeves is a **jumper**.

Kk

kangaroo

A **kangaroo** is an Australian animal. Baby **kangaroos** are carried in their mother's pouch.

key

You open a lock with a **key**.

king

A **king** is the head of a country.

kiss

The girl is giving the baby a **kiss**.

kite

The boy is flying his **kite**.
He must hold on to the string
of his **kite**.

kitten

A **kitten** is a young cat.

knee

Your leg bends in the middle
at the **knee**.

knife

We cut things with a **knife**.

Ll

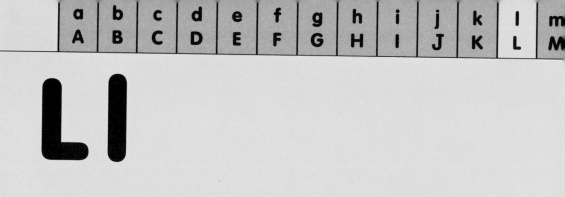

ladder

You climb a **ladder** to get up to high things.

ladybird

A **ladybird** is a tiny red or yellow insect with spots on its back.

lake

A **lake** is a lot of water with land all round it.

lamb

A **lamb** is a young sheep.

lamp

A **lamp** gives us light. When it gets dark, we switch on the **lamp**.

leaf

A **leaf** will grow on a tree or a plant.

leap-frog

It is fun to play **leap-frog**. In **leap-frog**, you leap over your friends' backs.

leg

We have two **legs**. The boy is waving one **leg** in the air.

lemon

A **lemon** is a yellow fruit with a bitter taste.

leopard

A **leopard** is a large, wild animal with a spotted coat.

letter

When we write a **letter**, we are sending a message to someone.

library

A **library** is a room or a building where books are kept.

lighthouse

A **lighthouse** is a tall building with a light on top to warn ships of danger.

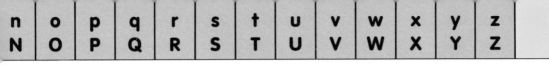

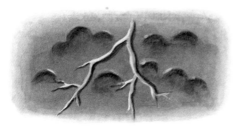

lightning

Lightning is the flash that we see in the sky during a thunderstorm.

lion

A **lion** is a fierce, wild animal. **Lions** are part of the cat family.

lizard

A **lizard** is an animal with short legs and a long tail.

lock

The cupboard has a **lock** on it. You need a key to un**lock** the cupboard.

locomotive

The machine that pulls a train is called a **locomotive**.

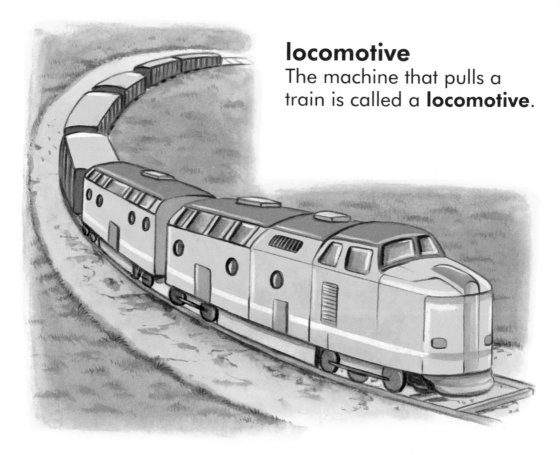

lollipop

A **lollipop** is a sweet on a stick. We lick a **lollipop**.

M m

machine

A **machine** is something that helps us to do work more easily. We clean clothes in a washing-**machine**.

magic

The man is doing **magic** tricks. It is difficult to understand how a **magic** trick works.

mask

The boy is wearing a **mask**. His face is covered with a **mask**.

mat

A **mat** is like a small rug.
We wipe our feet on a
door**mat**.

medicine

Medicine is something we
take to make us better when
we are not well.

mermaid

In stories, a **mermaid** is a
woman who lives in the sea.
She has a fish's tail instead
of legs.

milk

Milk is a white drink that
comes from cows.
Children drink a lot of **milk**.

mirror

A **mirror** is a piece of glass
that we can see ourselves in.

mole
A **mole** is a furry animal that lives underground.

moneybox
We keep our savings in a **moneybox**. Often a **moneybox** is a fat pig.

monkey
A **monkey** is a wild, furry animal. **Monkeys** are very good at climbing.

mountain
A hill that is very high is called a **mountain**.

mouse

A **mouse** is a tiny animal with a long tail. **Mice** have sharp teeth.

mouth

A **mouth** is the opening in our face. We talk and eat with our **mouths**.

mushroom

A **mushroom** is a small plant that grows in woods and fields. **Mushrooms** are shaped like little umbrellas.

music

Music is the nice sound you make when you sing. Guitar **music** also sounds good.

Nn

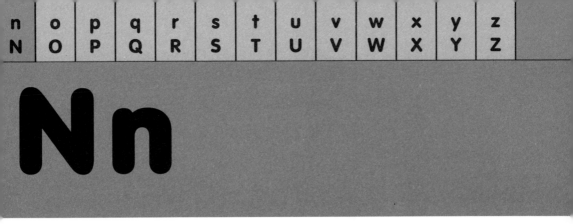

neck
The **neck** is the part of the body that joins the head to the shoulders. Giraffes have very long **necks**.

necklace
Some people wear a decoration called a **necklace** round their neck.

needle
We use a **needle** for sewing.

nest
Birds, and some other animals, make a cosy home called a **nest**.

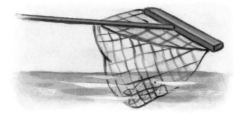

net
Sometimes a **net** is used for catching fish.

newt
A **newt** is like a lizard that lives partly in water.

nose
We breathe and smell through our **nose**.

nurse
A **nurse** looks after us when we are sick.

nuts
When we have taken off the hard shells, we can eat **nuts**.

Oo

oar

An **oar** is a long piece of wood with one flat end. We use **oars** to move a rowing boat.

ocean

An **ocean** is a very large sea. One **ocean** is the Atlantic **Ocean**.

octopus

An **octopus** lives in the sea. It has eight long legs with suckers on them.

onion

Onions are good to eat. We cry when we cut an **onion**.

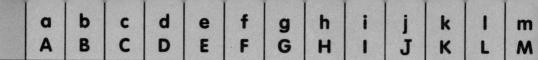

orange
Orange is a colour.
The boy's jumper is **orange**.

orange
An **orange** is a kind of fruit.
Oranges are sweet and
good to eat.

orchard
A field full of fruit trees is
called an **orchard**.

orchestra
A lot of people making
music together is called an
orchestra.

ostrich
The **ostrich** is the largest bird in the world.
An **ostrich** cannot fly.

otter
An **otter** is a brown, furry animal. **Otters** can swim well and they eat fish.

oven
We cook lots of things like cakes and biscuits in an **oven**.

overalls
We wear **overalls** when working, to keep our clothes clean.

owl
An **owl** is a bird with a big head and eyes. **Owls** can see well in the dark.

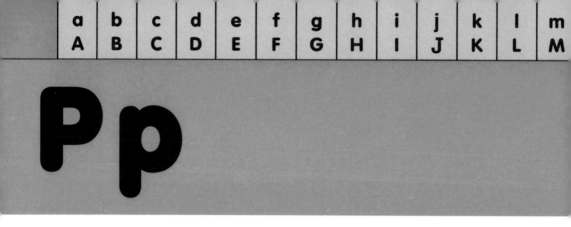

Pp

pail
Jack and Jill carried a **pail** of water. Another name for a **pail** is a bucket.

paint
We put **paint** on things to make them bright and pretty. **Paint** comes in cans.

pancake
A **pancake** is flat and round, and good to eat.

panda
A **panda** is a big, black and white bear.

parade

It is fun to watch a circus **parade**.

park

A **park** is a place with grass and trees, where anyone can play.

parrot

A **parrot** is a colourful bird. **Parrots** can learn to say some words.

party

At a **party**, we have lots of fun together. Usually, we have a **party** on our birthday.

paw

A **paw** is an animal's foot with claws. Dogs and cats have **paws**.

peacock

A **peacock** is a bird with a tail of colourful feathers.

pen

We can write and draw with a **pen**.

pets

Pets are animals that we keep as special friends.
A **pet** can be a dog, a cat, a rabbit, a canary or a goldfish.

piano

We can make music with a **piano**.

picnic

When we eat outdoors, we are having a **picnic**.

pie

A **pie** is filled with fruit or meat and cooked in the oven.

pig

A **pig** is a pink animal with a curly tail. We keep **pigs** on farms.

pigeon

A **pigeon** is a plump bird with short legs. **Pigeons** can find their way home from far away.

pilot

A **pilot** is the person who flies an aircraft.

pink

Pink is a colour.
The ballet shoes are **pink**.

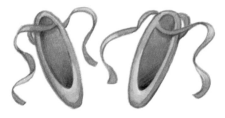

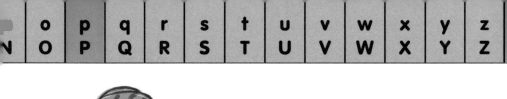

pirate

A **pirate** is someone who robs from ships.

pocket

A **pocket** is like a little bag in our clothes. We can keep lots of things in our **pockets**.

polar bear

A **polar bear** is a wild animal that lives in very cold places.

pond

A **pond** is a small patch of water. Sometimes we have a **pond** in the garden.

pony
A **pony** is like a little horse.

puppet
We play with a **puppet** by moving its strings. There are also **puppets** like gloves.

puppy
A **puppy** is a young dog.

purple
Purple is a colour.
The flowers are **purple**.

purse
We put money in a **purse** to keep it safe.

Qq

quack
Ducks **quack**. A **quack** is the sound they make.

queen
A **queen** is the head of a country. The wife of a king is also a **queen**.

quilt
A **quilt** is the warm, padded cover on our bed.

quiver
We carry arrows in a **quiver**.

Rr

rabbit

A **rabbit** is a small, furry animal with very long ears. A **rabbit** is sometimes called a bunny.

race

We have a **race** to see who is the fastest at something. The children are in a swimming **race**.

raft

A **raft** is a flat boat made out of wood.

railway

A **railway** is the rail track
that trains and trams run on.

rain

Rain falls on us from the
clouds. We get wet when it is
raining.

rainbow

When the sun shines after it
has rained, we sometimes
see a **rainbow** in the sky.

rattle

A baby will play with a
rattle. A **rattle** makes a
rattling noise.

red
Red is a colour.
The bus is **red**.

reindeer
A **reindeer** is an animal with very large horns.

ring
Sometimes we wear a **ring** on our finger. A **ring** is a circle.

river
A **river** is a large stream of moving water. Some **rivers** move slowly, some move fast.

robot
This toy **robot** is a machine in the shape of a person.

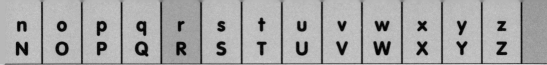

n	o	p	q	r	s	t	u	v	w	x	y	z
N	O	P	Q	R	S	T	U	V	W	X	Y	Z

rocket

A **rocket** shoots up into the air. It is fun to see **rockets** when there are fireworks.

rocking horse

When we are little, we can play on a **rocking horse**.

roller skates

We can move fast when we play on **roller skates**.

root

A **root** is the part of a tree or plant under the ground.

runway

Aircraft land and take off from a **runway**. A **runway** is a road for aircraft.

Ss

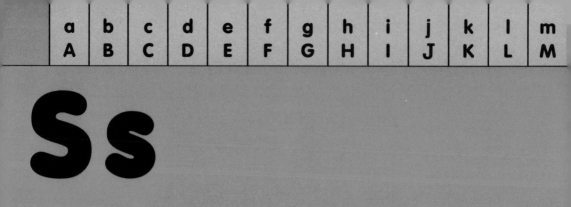

saddle
You sit in a **saddle** when you ride a horse.

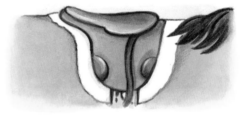

sail
The wind blows into a **sail** and moves the boat along.

salad
A **salad** is a mixture of vegetables or fruit. **Salads** are cold.

sandcastle
It is fun to build a **sandcastle** on the beach.

Santa Claus
Santa Claus brings us presents at Christmas.

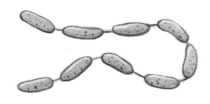

sausages
Here is a string of **sausages**. Most children enjoy eating **sausages**.

saw
A **saw** has a sharp, jagged edge. We cut things with a **saw**.

school
People go to **school** to learn things. Children learn to read and write at **school**.

scissors
Scissors will cut paper and cloth. We say that we have a pair of **scissors**.

sea
The **sea** is the water that covers most of the earth. **Sea** water is salty.

seal
A **seal** is an animal with fur and flippers. **Seals** spend most of their time in the sea.

seashell
We can find lots of **seashells** beside the sea. A little animal used to live in every **seashell**.

see-saw
The children are playing on a **see-saw**.

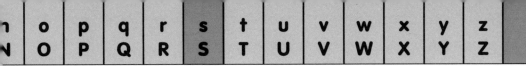

shadow
A light in front of us makes a **shadow** behind us.
A **shadow** is the dark shape we make in the light.

shark
A **shark** lives in the sea.
Some **sharks** eat people!

sheep
We keep **sheep** on farms.
Wool is made from a **sheep's** coat.

ship
We travel across the sea in a **ship**.
Some **ships** are very big.

shop
We can buy things in a **shop**.

shower
A **shower** sprays us with water so that we can wash ourselves.

signpost
A **signpost** points the way to somewhere.

singer
Someone who makes music with their voice is a **singer**.

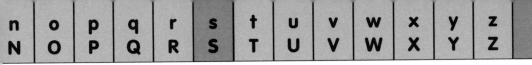

n	o	p	q	r	s	t	u	v	w	x	y	z
N	O	P	Q	R	S	T	U	V	W	X	Y	Z

skateboard

A **skateboard** is a board with wheels on it. You can move about and do tricks on a **skateboard**.

skeleton

Our **skeleton** is made up of all the bones in our body.

sleep

We go to bed to **sleep**. When we are tired, we need to have a **sleep**.

sleigh

We travel over the snow in a **sleigh**. Santa uses a **sleigh** to deliver presents.

smoke

Smoke is the dark cloud that we see when something is burning.

snail

A **snail** is a small animal with a shell on its back. **Snails** move very slowly.

snakes

Snakes are long, thin animals without legs. A **snake** slides along the ground.

snow

When it is cold, flakes of frozen water called **snow** fall from the sky.

spider

A **spider** is a little animal with eight legs.
Spiders make a web to catch their food.

squirrel

A **squirrel** is a red or grey animal with a bushy tail.
Squirrels live in trees.

stars

We can see lots of tiny lights in the sky at night. They are the **stars**.

starfish

A **starfish** is a star-shaped fish. You will sometimes find one at the edge of the sea.

steeple

A **steeple** is the high, pointed top of a church.

storm

It is a **storm** when there are strong winds and heavy rain.

street

A road with houses or shops along it is a **street**.

submarine

A **submarine** is a boat that can go under the water.

sunflower

A **sunflower** is a large, golden flower. A **sunflower** always faces the sun.

supermarket

A very big shop is called a **supermarket**.

swan

A **swan** is a big, white bird with a very long neck.

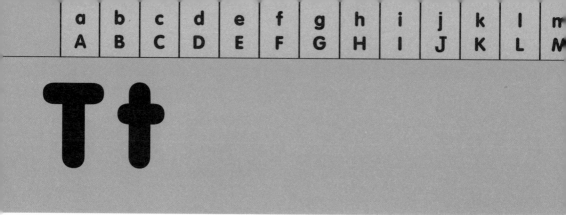

Tt

tail

A **tail** is the end of something.
Most animals have **tails**.

tambourine

Sometimes we make music with a **tambourine**.

tangle

The dogs' leads are in a **tangle**. They are all knotted together.

taxi

A **taxi** is like a car that will take us places for money.
Taxi is short for **taxi**cab.

teacher

The **teacher** teaches us things at school. We learn things from the **teacher**.

Teddy bear

A **Teddy bear** is soft and warm.

telephone

We talk on the **telephone** to someone far away. A **telephone** is a **phone**.

television

Television shows us pictures in our homes from far away.

tent
When we are camping, we sleep in a **tent**.

theatre
We go to the **theatre** to see actors, and to hear music.

thermometer
When we are not well, a **thermometer** measures how hot we are.

thumb
On each hand, we have a **thumb** and four other fingers.

tiger
A **tiger** is a big, wild animal with a striped coat.

toes

We have five **toes** on the end of each foot.

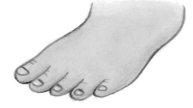

tomato

A **tomato** is a soft red fruit. We eat **tomatoes** raw or cooked.

tools

Tools help us to do work. A screwdriver is a **tool**.

tooth

A **tooth** is one of the hard white bones in our mouth. We bite things with our **teeth**.

tortoise
A **tortoise** is a slow-moving animal with a hard shell on its back.

tower
The walls of a castle have **towers** at each corner.
A **tower** is a tall, narrow building.

toys
Toy boats, **toy** ducks, and **toy** drums are all **toys**.

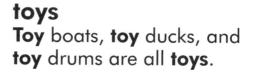

tractor
A **tractor** can pull heavy things over muddy ground.

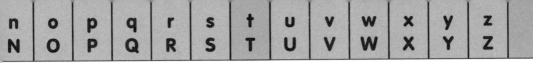

train

A **train** is pulled by a locomotive. Sometimes there are lots of wagons in a **train**.

tree

A **tree** is a very big plant. **Trees** have branches and leaves.

truck

Lots of things are carried by road in a **truck**.

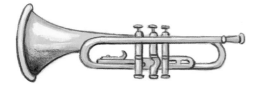

trumpet

We can make music by blowing a **trumpet**.

tunnel

A **tunnel** is a passage under the ground.

a	b	c	d	e	f	g	h	i	j	k	l	m
A	B	C	D	E	F	G	H	I	J	K	L	M

Uu

umbrella
An **umbrella** will keep us dry when it rains.

unicorn
In fairy-tales, a **unicorn** is a magic animal, like a horse with one horn on its head.

uniform
A **uniform** is a set of special clothes that some people wear. A nurse wears a **uniform**.

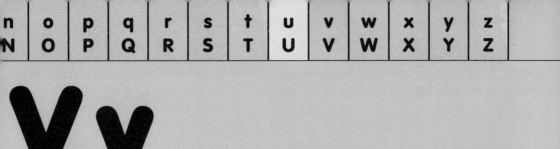

n	o	p	q	r	s	t	u	v	w	x	y	z
N	O	P	Q	R	S	T	U	V	W	X	Y	Z

Vv

vacuum cleaner
A **vacuum cleaner** is a machine that sucks up dirt.

valley
A **valley** is the low piece of land between hills. Often a river goes through a **valley**.

van
A small truck for delivering things is called a **van**.

vase
We put flowers in a **vase**.

vegetables

Vegetables are plants that we grow for food. We eat lots of **vegetables**. They are good for us.

violin

We can make music on a **violin** by rubbing a stick called a bow against the **violin** strings.

voice

When we sing, we are using our **voice**. We also use our **voice** to speak.

W w

wagon
A **wagon** is a cart for carrying heavy loads. Sometimes a **wagon** is pulled by horses.

waist
Our **waist** is in the middle of our body. Our body bends at the **waist**.

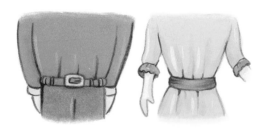

walrus
A **walrus** is a big sea animal with two long tusks.

watch
A **watch** is like a small clock that we wear on our arm.

waterfall

A stream of water falling over a cliff is called a **waterfall**.

well

A **well** is a deep hole in the ground with water in it.

whale

A **whale** is a big animal that lives in the sea.

wheelbarrow

We can use a **wheelbarrow** in the garden.
A **wheelbarrow** has two long handles and one wheel.

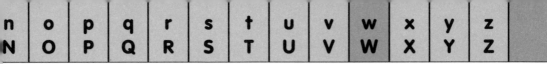

n	o	p	q	r	s	t	u	v	w	x	y	z
N	O	P	Q	R	S	T	U	V	W	X	Y	Z

wigwam

A **wigwam** is a kind of tent that some American Indians used to live in.

windmill

The wind blows round the sails of a **windmill**. **Windmills** are machines that can lift water.

wing

The **wing** is the part of a bird that it uses to fly. Birds have two **wings**.

woodpecker

A **woodpecker** is a bird that pecks wood. You can often hear a **woodpecker** tapping on a tree.

worm

A **worm** is like a little snake that lives in the earth.

wrist

Our **wrist** joins our hand to our arm. We have two **wrists**.

Xx

x-ray

A picture of the inside of our body is called an **x-ray**.

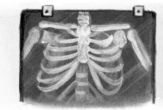

xylophone

We play a **xylophone** to make music.

Yy

yacht
A boat with large sails is called a **yacht**.

yawn
We make a **yawn** when we are tired. When we **yawn** we open our mouth wide.

yellow
Yellow is a colour. The little bird is **yellow**.

yo-yo
A **yo-yo** is a toy. We spin a **yo-yo** up and down.

a	b	c	d	e	f	g	h	i	j	k	l	m
A	B	C	D	E	F	G	H	I	J	K	L	M

n	o	p	q	r	s	t
N	O	P	Q	R	S	T

u	v	w	x	y	z
U	V	W	X	Y	Z

Zz

zebra

A **zebra** is a wild animal like a striped horse.

zip

A **zip** fastens parts of our clothes together. Sometimes we have a **zip** at the front of our jacket.

First Published 1993

Published by
Brown Watson Ltd
The Old Mill
76 Fleckney Road
Kibworth Beauchamp
Leicestershire, England